'The Arg were terrified at the sight. But Jason planting his feet apart stood to receive them, as a reef in the sea confronts the tossing billows in a gale.'

APOLLONIUS OF RHODES
Lived in the 3rd century BCE
Dates and location of birth and death unknown

Taken from E. V. Rieu's translation of *The Voyage of Argo*,
first published in 1959.

APOLLONIUS OF RHODES IN PENGUIN CLASSICS
The Voyage of Argo

APOLLONIUS OF RHODES

Jason and Medea

Translated by
E. V. Rieu

PENGUIN BOOKS

PENGUIN CLASSICS

Published by the Penguin Group
Penguin Books Ltd, 80 Strand, London WC2R ORL, England
Penguin Group (USA) Inc., 375 Hudson Street, New York, New York 10014, USA
Penguin Group (Canada), 90 Eglinton Avenue East, Suite 700, Toronto, Ontario,
Canada M4P 2Y3 (a division of Pearson Penguin Canada Inc.)
Penguin Ireland, 25 St Stephen's Green, Dublin 2, Ireland
(a division of Penguin Books Ltd)
Penguin Group (Australia), 707 Collins Street, Melbourne, Victoria 3008, Australia
(a division of Pearson Australia Group Pty Ltd)
Penguin Books India Pvt Ltd, 11 Community Centre, Panchsheel Park,
New Delhi – 110 017, India
Penguin Group (NZ), 67 Apollo Drive, Rosedale, Auckland 0632, New Zealand
(a division of Pearson New Zealand Ltd)
Penguin Books (South Africa) (Pty) Ltd, Block D, Rosebank Office Park,
181 Jan Smuts Avenue, Parktown North, Gauteng 2193, South Africa

Penguin Books Ltd, Registered Offices: 80 Strand, London WC2R ORL, England

www.penguin.com

This selection published in Penguin Classics 2015
001

Translation copyright © E. V. Rieu, 1959, 1971

Set in 9.5/13 pt Baskerville 10 Pro
Typeset by Jouve (UK), Milton Keynes
Printed in Great Britain by Clays Ltd, St Ives plc

A CIP catalogue record for this book is available from the British Library

ISBN: 978-0-141-39794-8

www.greenpenguin.co.uk

Come, Erato, come lovely Muse, stand by me and take up the tale. How did Medea's passion help Jason to bring back the fleece to Iolcus? You that share Aphrodite's powers must surely know; you that fill virgin hearts with love's inquietude and bear a name that speaks of love's delights.

We left the young lords lying there concealed among the rushes. But ambushed though they were, Here and Athene saw them and at once withdrew from Zeus and the rest of the immortal gods into a private room to talk the matter over.

Here began by sounding Athene. 'Daughter of Zeus,' she said, 'let me hear you first. What are we to do? Will you think of some ruse that might enable them to carry off Aeëtes' golden fleece to Hellas? Or should they speak him fair in the hope of winning his consent? I know the man is thoroughly intractable. But all the same, no method of approach should be neglected.'

'Here,' said Athene quickly, 'you have put to me the very questions I have been turning over in my mind. But

I must admit that, though I have racked my brains, I have failed so far to think of any scheme that might commend itself to the noble lords.'

For a while the two goddesses sat staring at the floor, each lost in her own perplexities. Here was the first to break the silence; an idea had struck her. 'Listen,' she said. 'We must have a word with Aphrodite. Let us go together and ask her to persuade her boy, if that is possible, to loose an arrow at Aeëtes' daughter, Medea of the many spells, and make her fall in love with Jason. I am sure that with her help he will succeed in bearing off the fleece to Hellas.'

This solution of their problem pleased Athene, who smilingly replied: 'Sprung as I am from Zeus, I have never felt the arrows of the Boy, and of love-charms I know nothing. However, if you yourself are satisfied with the idea, I will certainly go with you. But when we meet her you must be the one to speak.'

The two goddesses rose at once and made their way to the palace of Aphrodite, which her lame consort Hephaestus had built for her when he took her as his bride from the hands of Zeus. They entered the courtyard and paused below the veranda of the room where the goddess slept with her lord and master. Hephaestus himself had gone early to his forge and anvils in a vast cavern on a floating island, where he used to turn out all kinds of curious metalwork with the aid of fire and bellows; and Cypris, left at home alone, was sitting on an inlaid chair which faced the door. She had let her hair fall down on her white shoulders and was combing it with a golden comb before plaiting the long tresses. But when she saw the goddesses outside she stopped and called them in; and she rose to meet them and settled them in easy chairs before resuming her own seat. Then she bound up the uncombed locks with both hands, gave her visitors a smile, and spoke with mock humility:

'Ladies, you honour me! What brings you here after so long? We have seen little of you in the past. To what then do I owe a visit from the greatest goddesses of all?'

'This levity of yours,' said Here, 'is ill-timed. We two are facing a disaster. At this very moment the lord Jason and his friends are riding at anchor in the River Phasis. They have come to fetch the fleece, and since the time for action is at hand, we are gravely concerned for all of them, particularly Aeson's son. For him, I am prepared to fight with all my might and main, and I will save him, even if he sails to Hell to free Ixion from his brazen chains. For I will not have King Pelias boasting that he has escaped his evil doom, insolent Pelias, who left me out when he made offerings to the gods. Besides which I have been very fond of Jason ever since the time when I was putting human charity on trial and as he came home from the chase he met me at the mouth of the Anaurus. The river was in spate, for all the mountains and their high spurs were under snow and cataracts were roaring down their sides. I was disguised as an old woman and he took pity on me, lifted me up, and carried me across the flood on his shoulders. For that, I will never cease to honour him. But Pelias will not be brought to book for his outrageous conduct unless you yourself make it possible for Jason to return.'

Here had finished; but for a time words failed the Lady of Cyprus. The sight of Here begging her for favours struck her with awe; and her answer when it came was gracious. 'Queen of goddesses,' she said, 'regard me as the meanest creature in the world if I fail you in your need. Whatever I can say or do, whatever strength these feeble hands possess, is at your service. Moreover I expect no recompense.'

Here, choosing her words with care, replied: 'We are not asking you to use your hands: force is not needed. All we require of you is quietly to tell your boy to use his wizardry and make Aeëtes' daughter fall in love with Jason. With Medea on his side he should find it easy to carry off the golden fleece and make his way back to Iolcus. She is something of a witch herself.'

'But ladies,' said Cypris, speaking now to both of them, 'he is far more likely to obey you than me. There is no reverence in him, but faced by you he might display some spark of decent feeling. He certainly pays no attention to me: he defies me and always does the opposite of what I say. In fact I am so worn out by his naughtiness that I have half a mind to break his bow and wicked arrows in his very sight, remembering how he threatened me with them in one of his moods. He said, "If you don't keep your hands off me while I can still control my temper, you can blame yourself for the consequences." '

Here and Athene smiled at this and exchanged glances. But Aphrodite was hurt. She said: 'Other people find my troubles amusing. I really should not speak of them to all and sundry; it is enough for me to know them. However, as you have both set your hearts on it, I will try and coax my boy. He will not refuse.'

Here took Aphrodite's slender hand in hers and with a sweet smile replied: 'Very well, Cytherea. Play your part, just as you say; but quickly, please. And do not scold or argue with your child when he annoys you. He will improve by and by.'

With that she rose to go. Athene followed her, and the pair left for home. Cypris too set out, and after searching up and down Olympus for her boy, found him far away in the fruit-laden orchard of Zeus. With him was Ganymede, whose beauty had so captivated Zeus that he took him up to heaven to live with the immortals. The two lads, who had much in common, were playing with golden knuckle-bones. Eros, the greedy boy, was standing there with a whole handful of them clutched to his breast and a happy flush mantling his cheeks. Near by sat Ganymede, hunched up, silent and disconsolate, with only two left. He threw these for what they were worth in quick succession and was furious when Eros laughed. Of course he lost them both immediately – they joined the rest. So he went off in despair with empty hands and did not notice the goddess's approach.

Aphrodite came up to her boy, took his chin in her hand, and said: 'Why this triumphant smile, you rascal? I do believe you won the game unfairly by cheating a beginner. But listen now. Will you be good and do me a favour I am going to ask of you? Then I will give you one of Zeus's lovely toys, the one that his fond nurse Adresteia made for him in the Idaean cave when he was still a child and liked to play. It is a perfect ball; Hephaestus himself could not make you a better toy. It is made of golden hoops laced together all the way round with double stitching; but the seams are hidden by a winding, dark blue band. When you throw it up, it will leave a fiery trail behind it like a meteor in the sky. That is what I'll give you, if you let fly an arrow at Aeëtes' girl and make her fall in love with Jason. But you must act at once, or I may not be so generous.'

When he heard this, Eros was delighted. He threw down all his toys, flung his arms round his mother and hung on to her skirt with both hands, imploring her to let him have the ball at once. But she gently refused, and drawing him towards her, held him close and kissed his cheeks. Then with a smile she said, 'By your own dear head and mine, I swear I will not disappoint you. You shall have the gift when you have shot an arrow into Medea's heart.'

Eros gathered up his knuckle-bones, counted them all

carefully, and put them in the fold of his mother's shining robe. Fetching his quiver from where it leant against a tree, he slung it on his shoulder with a golden strap, picked up his crooked bow, and made his way through the luxuriant orchard of Zeus's palace. Then he passed through the celestial gates of Olympus, where a pathway for the gods leads down, and twin poles, earth's highest points, soar up in lofty pinnacles that catch the first rays of the risen sun. And as he swept on through the boundless air he saw an ever-changing scene beneath him, here the life-supporting land with its peopled cities and its sacred rivers, here mountain peaks, and here the all-encircling sea.

Meanwhile the Argonauts were sitting in conference on the benches of their ship where it lay hidden in the marshes of the river. Each man had taken his own seat, and Jason, who was speaking, was faced by row upon row of quiet listeners. 'My friends,' he said, 'I am going to tell you what action I myself should like to take, though its success depends on you. Sharing the danger as we do, we share the right of speech; and I warn the man who keeps his mouth shut when he ought to speak his mind that he will be the one to wreck our enterprise.

'I ask you all to stay quietly on board with your arms ready, while I go up to Aeëtes' palace with the sons of Phrixus and two other men. When I see him I intend to parley with him first and find out whether he means to treat us as friends and let us have the golden fleece, or dismiss us with contempt, relying on his own power. Warned thus, by the man himself, of any evil thoughts he may be entertaining, we will decide whether to face him in the field or find some way of getting what we want without recourse to arms. We ought not to use force to rob him of his own without so much as seeing what a few words may do; it would be much better to talk to him first and try to win him over. Speech, by smoothing the way, often succeeds where forceful measures might have failed. Remember too that Aeëtes welcomed the admirable Phrixus when he fled from a stepmother's treachery and a father who had planned to sacrifice him. Every man on earth, even the greatest rogue, fears Zeus the god of hospitality and keeps his laws.'

With one accord the young men approved the lord Jason's plan, and no one having risen to suggest another, he asked the sons of Phrixus, with Telamon and Augeias, to accompany him and himself took the Wand of Hermes in his hand. Leaving the ship they came to dry land beyond the reeds and water and passed on to the high ground of the plain which bears the name of Circe. Here osiers and willows stand in rows, with corpses dangling on ropes from their highest branches. To this day the Colchians would think it sacrilege to burn the bodies of their men. They never bury them or raise a mound above them, but wrap them in untanned oxhide and hang them up on trees at a distance from the town. Thus, since it is

8

their custom to bury women, earth and air play equal parts in the disposal of their dead.

While Jason and his friends were on their way, Here had a kindly thought for them. She covered the whole town with mist so that they might reach Aeëtes' house unseen by any of the numerous Colchians. But as soon as they had come in from the country and reached the palace she dispersed the mist. At the entrance they paused for a moment to marvel at the king's courtyard with its wide gates, the rows of soaring columns round the palace walls, and high over all the marble cornice resting on triglyphs of bronze. They crossed the threshold of the court unchallenged. Near by, cultivated vines covered with greenery rose high in the air and underneath them four perennial springs gushed up. These were Hephaestus' work. One flowed with milk, and one with wine, the third with fragrant oil, while the fourth was a fountain of water which grew warm when the Pleiades set, but changed at their rising and bubbled up from the hollow rock as cold as ice. Such were the marvels that Hephaestus the great Engineer had contrived for the palace of Cytaean Aeëtes. He had also made him bulls with feet of bronze and bronze mouths from which the breath came out in flame, blazing and terrible. And he had forged a plough of indurated steel, all in one piece, as a thank-offering to Helios, who had taken him up in his chariot when he sank exhausted on the battlefield of Phlegra.

There was also an inner court, with many well-made folding doors leading to various rooms, and decorated galleries to right and left. Higher buildings stood at angles to this court on either side. In one of them, the highest, King Aeëtes lived with his queen; in another, his son Apsyrtus, whom a Caucasian nymph named Asterodeia had borne to him before he married Eidyia, the youngest daughter of Tethys and Ocean. 'Phaëthon' was the nickname that the young Colchians gave Apsyrtus because he outshone them all.

The other buildings housed the maidservants and Chalciope and Medea, the two daughters of Aeëtes. At the moment, Medea was going from room to room to find her sister. The goddess Here had kept her in the house, though as a rule she did not spend her time at home, but was busy all day in the temple of Hecate, of whom she was priestess. When she saw the men she gave a cry; Chalciope heard it, and her maids dropped their yarn and spindles on the floor and all ran out of doors.

When Chalciope saw her sons among the strangers, she lifted up her hands for joy. They greeted her in the same fashion and then in their happiness embraced her. But she had her moan to make. 'So after all,' she said, 'you were not allowed to roam so very far from your neglected mother: Fate turned you back. But how I have suffered! This mad desire of yours for Hellas! This blind obedience to your dying father's wishes! What misery, what heartache, they brought me! Why should you go to the city of

Orchomenus, whoever he may be, abandoning your wid-
owed mother for the sake of your grandfather's estate?'

Last of all, Aeëtes with his queen, Eidyia, who had
heard Chalciope speaking, came out of the house. And
at once the whole courtyard was astir. A number of his
men busied themselves over the carcass of a large bull;
others chopped firewood; others heated water for the
baths. Not one of them took a rest: they were working
for the king.

Meanwhile Eros, passing through the clear air, had
arrived unseen and bent on mischief, like a gadfly setting
out to plague the grazing heifers, the fly that cowherds
call the breese. In the porch, under the lintel of the door,
he quickly strung his bow and from his quiver took a new
arrow, fraught with pain. Still unobserved, he ran across
the threshold glancing around him sharply. Then he
crouched low at Jason's feet, fitted the notch to the middle
of the string, and drawing the bow as far as his hands
would stretch, shot at Medea. And her heart stood still.

With a happy laugh Eros sped out of the high-roofed
hall on his way back, leaving his shaft deep in the girl's
breast, hot as fire. Time and again she darted a bright
glance at Jason. All else was forgotten. Her heart, brimful
of this new agony, throbbed within her and overflowed
with the sweetness of the pain.

A working woman, rising before dawn to spin and need-
ing light in her cottage room, piles brushwood on a
smouldering log, and the whole heap kindled by the little

11

brand goes up in a mighty blaze. Such was the fire of Love, stealthy but all-consuming, that swept through Medea's heart. In the turmoil of her soul, her soft cheeks turned from rose to white and white to rose.

By now the servants had prepared a banquet for the newcomers, who gladly sat down to it after refreshing themselves in warm baths. When they had enjoyed the food and drink, Aeëtes put some questions to his grandsons:

'Sons of my daughter and of Phrixus, the most deserving guest I have ever entertained, how is it that you are back in Aea? Did some misadventure cut your journey short? You refused to listen when I told you what a long way you had to go. But I knew; for I myself was whirled along it in the chariot of my father Helios, when he took my sister Circe to the Western Land and we reached the coast of Tyrrhenia, where she still lives, far, far indeed from Colchis. But enough of that. Tell me plainly what befell you, who your companions are, and where you disembarked.'

To answer these questions, Argus stepped out in front of his brothers, being the eldest of the four. His heart misgave him for Jason and his mission; but he did his best to conciliate the king. 'My lord,' he said, 'that ship of ours soon fell to pieces in a storm. We hung on to one of her planks and were cast ashore on the Island of Ares in the pitch-dark night. But Providence looked after us: there was not a sign of the War-god's birds, who used to haunt the desert isle. They were driven off by these men, who had landed on the previous day and been detained there by the will of Zeus in pity for ourselves – or was it only chance? In any case, they gave us plenty of food and clothing directly they heard the illustrious name of Phrixus, and your own, my lord, since it was your city they were bound for. As to their purpose, I will be frank with you. A certain king, wishing to banish and dispossess this man because he is the most powerful of the Aeolids, has sent him here on a desperate venture, maintaining that the House of Aeolus will not escape the inexorable wrath of Zeus, the heavy burden of their guilt, and vengeance for the sufferings of Phrixus, till the fleece returns to Hellas. The ship that brought him was built by Pallas Athene on altogether different lines from the Colchian craft, the rottenest of which, as luck would have it, fell to us. For *she* was smashed to pieces by the wind and waves, whereas the bolts of *Argo* hold her together in any gale that blows, and she runs as sweetly when the crew are tugging at the oars as she does before the wind. This ship he manned with the pick of all Achaea, and in her he has come to your city, touching at many ports and crossing formidable seas, in the hope that you will let him have the fleece. But it must be as you wish. He has not come here to force your hand. On the contrary, he is willing to repay you amply for the gift by reducing for you your bitter enemies, the Sauromatae, of whom I told him. But now you may wish to know the names and lineage of your visitors. Let me tell you. Here is the man to whom the others rallied from all parts of Hellas, Jason son of Aeson, Cretheus' son. He must be a kinsman of our own on the father's side, if he is a grandson of Cretheus, for Cretheus and Athamas were both sons of Aeolus, and our father Phrixus was a son of Athamas. Next, and in case you have heard that we have a son of Helios with us, behold the man, Augeias. And this is Telamon, son of the illustrious Aeacus, a son of Zeus himself. Much the same is true of all the rest of Jason's followers. They are all sons or grandsons of immortal gods.'

The king was filled with rage as he listened to Argus. And now, in a towering passion, he gave vent to his displeasure, the brunt of which fell on the sons of Chalciope, whom he held responsible for the presence of the rest. His eyes blazed with fury as he burst into speech:

'You scoundrels! Get out of my sight at once. Get out of my country, you and your knavish tricks, before you meet a Phrixus and a fleece you will not relish. It was no fleece that brought you and your confederates from Hellas, but a plot to seize my sceptre and my royal power. If you had not eaten at my table first, I would tear your tongues out and chop off your hands, both of them, and send you back with nothing but your feet, to teach you to think twice before starting on another expedition. As for all that about the blessed gods, it is nothing but a pack of lies.'

Telamon's gorge rose at this outburst from the angry

king, and he was on the point of flinging back defiance, to his own undoing, when he was checked by Jason, who forestalled him with a more politic reply.

'My lord,' he said, 'pray overlook our show of arms. We have not come to your city and palace with any such designs as you suspect. Nor have we predatory aims. Who of his own accord would brave so vast a sea to lay his hands on other people's goods? No; it was Destiny and the cruel orders of a brutal king that sent me here. Be generous to your suppliants, and I will make all Hellas ring with the glory of your name. And by way of more immediate recompense, we are prepared to take the field in your behalf against the Sauromatae or any other tribe you may wish to subdue.'

Jason's obsequious address had no effect. The king was plunged in sullen cogitation, wondering whether to leap up and kill them on the spot or to put their powers to the proof. He ended by deciding for a test and said to Jason:

'Sir, there is no need for me to hear you out. If you are really children of the gods or have other grounds for approaching me as equals in the course of your piratical adventure, I will let you have the golden fleece – that is, if you still want it when I have put you to the proof. For I am not like your overlord in Hellas, as you describe him; I am not inclined to be ungenerous to men of rank.

'I propose to test your courage and abilities by setting you a task which, though formidable, is not beyond the strength of my two hands. Grazing on the plain of Ares,

15

I have a pair of bronze-footed and fire-breathing bulls. These I yoke and drive over the hard fallow of the plain, quickly ploughing a four-acre field up to the ridge at either end. Then I sow the furrows, not with corn, but with the teeth of a monstrous serpent, which presently come up in the form of armed men, whom I cut down and kill with my spear as they rise up against me on all sides. It is morning when I yoke my team and by evening I have done my harvesting. That is what I do. If you, sir, can do as well, you may carry off the fleece to your king's palace on the very same day. If not, you shall not have it – do not deceive yourself. It would be wrong for a brave man to truckle to a coward.'

Jason listened to this with his eyes fixed on the floor; and when the king had finished, he sat there just as he was, without a word, resourceless in the face of his dilemma. For a long time he turned the matter over in his mind, unable boldly to accept a task so clearly fraught with peril. But at last he gave the king an answer which he thought would serve:

'Your Majesty, right is on your side and you leave me no escape whatever. Therefore I will take up your challenge, in spite of its preposterous terms, and though I may be courting death. Men serve no harsher mistress than Necessity, who drives me now and forced me to come here at another king's behest.'

He spoke in desperation and was little comforted by

Aeëtes' sinister reply: 'Go now and join your company: you have shown your relish for the task. But if you hesitate to yoke the bulls or shirk the deadly harvesting, I will take the matter up myself in a manner calculated to make others shrink from coming here and pestering their betters.'

He had made his meaning clear, and Jason rose from his chair. Augeias and Telamon followed him at once, and so did Argus, but without his brothers, whom he had warned by a nod to stay there for the time being. As the party went out of the hall, Jason's comeliness and charm singled him out from all the rest; and Medea, plucking her bright veil aside, turned wondering eyes upon him. Her heart smouldered with pain and as he passed from sight her soul crept out of her, as in a dream, and fluttered in his steps.

They left the palace with heavy hearts. Meanwhile Chalciope, to save herself from Aeëtes' wrath, had hastily withdrawn to her own room together with her sons. Medea too retired, a prey to all the inquietude that Love awakens. The whole scene was still before her eyes – how Jason looked, the clothes he wore, the things he said, the way he sat, and how he walked to the door. It seemed to her, as she reviewed these images, that there was nobody like Jason. His voice and the honey-sweet words that he had used still rang in her ears. But she feared for him. She was afraid that the bulls or Aeëtes with his own hands might kill him; and she mourned him as one already dead. The pity of it overwhelmed her; a round tear ran down her cheek; and weeping quietly she voiced her woes:

'What is the meaning of this grief? Hero or villain (and why should I care which?) the man is going to his death. Well, let him go! And yet I wish he had been spared. Yes, sovran Lady Hecate, this is my prayer. Let him live to reach his home. But if he must be conquered by the bulls, may he first learn that I for one do not rejoice in his cruel fate.'

While Medea thus tormented herself, Jason was listening to some advice from Argus, who had waited to address him till the people and the town were left behind and the party were retracing their steps across the plain.

'My lord,' he said, 'I have a plan to suggest. You will not like it; but in a crisis no expedient should be left untried. You have heard me speak of a young woman who practises witchcraft under the tutelage of the goddess Hecate. If we could win her over, we might banish from our minds all fear of your defeat in the ordeal. I am only afraid that my mother may not support me in this scheme. Nevertheless, since we all stand to lose our lives together, I will go back and sound her.'

'My friend,' said Jason, responding to the good will shown by Argus, 'if you are satisfied, then I have no objections. Go back at once and seek your mother's aid, feeling your way with care. But oh, how bleak the prospect is, with our one hope of seeing home again in women's hands!'

Soon after this they reached the marsh. Their comrades, when they saw them coming up, greeted them with cheerful enquiries, which Jason answered in a gloomy vein. 'Friends,' he said, 'if I were to answer all your questions, we should never finish; but the cruel king has definitely set his face against us. He said he had a couple of bronze-footed and fire-breathing bulls grazing on the plain of Ares, and told me to plough a four-acre field with these. He will give me seed from a serpent's jaws which will produce a crop of earthborn men in panoplies of bronze. And I have got to kill them before the day is done. That is my task. I straightway undertook it, for I had no choice.'

The task, as Jason had described it, seemed so impossible to all of them that for a while they stood there without a sound or word, looking at one another in impotent despair. But at last Peleus took heart and spoke out to his fellow chieftains: 'The time has come. We must confer and settle what to do. Not that debate will help us much: I would rather trust to strength of arm. Jason, my lord, if you fancy the adventure and mean to yoke Aeëtes' bulls you will naturally keep your promise and prepare. But if you have the slightest fear that your nerve may fail you, do not force yourself. And you need not sit there looking round for someone else. I, for one, am willing. The worst that I shall suffer will be death.'

So said the son of Aeacus. Telamon too was stirred and eagerly leapt up; next Idas, full of lofty thoughts; then

Castor and Polydeuces; and with them one who was already numbered with the men of might though the down was scarcely showing on his cheeks, Meleager son of Oeneus, his heart uplifted by the courage that dares all. But the others made no move, leaving it to these; and Argus addressed the six devoted men:

'My friends, you certainly provide us with a last resource. But I have some hopes of timely help that may be coming from my mother. So I advise you, keen as you are, to do as you did earlier and wait here in the ship for a little while – it is always better to think twice before one throws away one's life for nothing. There is a girl living in Aeëtes' palace whom the goddess Hecate has taught to handle with extraordinary skill all the magic herbs that grow on dry land or in running water. With these she can put out a raging fire, she can stop rivers as they roar in spate, arrest a star, and check the movement of the sacred moon. We thought of her as we made our way down here from the palace. My mother, her own sister, might persuade her to be our ally in the hour of trial; and with your approval I am prepared to go back to Aeëtes' palace this very day and see what I can do. Who knows? Some friendly Power may come to my assistance.'

So said Argus. And the gods were kind: they sent them a sign. In her terror, a timid dove, hotly pursued by a great hawk, dropped straight down into Jason's lap, while the hawk fell impaled on the mascot at the stern. Mopsus at once made the omens clear to all:

'It is for you, my friends, that Heaven has designed this portent. We could construe it in no better way than by approaching the girl with every plea we can devise. And I do not think she will refuse, if Phineus was right when he told us that our safety lay in Aphrodite's care; for this gentle bird whose life was spared belongs to her. May all turn out as I foresee, reading the omens with my inward eye. And so, my friends, let us invoke Cytherea's aid and put ourselves at once in the hands of Argus.'

The young men applauded, remembering what Phineus had told them. But there was one dissentient voice, and that a loud one. Idas leapt up in a towering rage and shouted: 'For shame! Have we come here to trot along with women, calling on Aphrodite to support us, instead of the mighty god of battle? Do you look to doves and hawks to get you out of trouble? Well, please yourselves! Forget that you are fighters. Pay court to girls and turn their silly heads.'

This tirade from Idas was received by many of his comrades with muttered resentment, though no one took the floor to answer him back. He sat down in high dudgeon, and Jason rose immediately to give them his decision and his orders. 'We are all agreed,' he said. 'Argus sets out from the ship. And we ourselves will now make fast with hawsers from the river to the shore, where anyone can see us. We certainly ought not to hide here any longer as though we were afraid of fighting.'

With that, he despatched Argus on his way back to the

town; and the crew, taking their orders from Aeson's son, hauled the anchor-stones on board and rowed *Argo* close to dry land, a little way from the marsh.

At the same time Aeëtes, meaning to play the Minyae false and do them grievous injury, summoned the Colchians to assemble, not in his palace, but at another spot where meetings had been held before. He declared that as soon as the bulls had destroyed the man who had taken up his formidable challenge, he would strip a forest hill of brushwood and burn the ship with every man on board, to cure them once for all of the intolerable airs they gave themselves, these enterprising buccaneers. It was true that he had welcomed Phrixus to his palace, but whatever the man's plight, he certainly would not have done so, though he had never known a foreigner so gentle and so well-conducted, if Zeus himself had not sent Hermes speeding down from heaven to see that he met with a sympathetic host. Much less should pirates landing in his country be left unpunished, men whose sole concern it was to get their hands on other people's goods, to lie in ambush plotting a sudden stroke, to sally out, cry havoc, and raid the farmers' yards. Moreover, Phrixus' sons should make him suitable amends for coming back in league with a gang of ruffians to hurl him from the throne. The crazy fools! But it all chimed in with an ugly hint he had had long ago from his father Helios, warning him to beware of treasonable plots and evil machinations in his own family. So, to complete their chastisement, he would pack them off to Achaea, just as they and their father had wished; and that was surely far enough. As for his daughters, he had not the slightest fear of treachery from them. Nor from his son Apsyrtus; only Chalciope's sons were involved in the mischief. The angry king ended by informing his people of the drastic measures that he had in mind, and ordering them, with many threats, to watch the ship and the men themselves so that no one should escape his doom.

By now Argus had reached the palace and was urging his mother with every argument at his command to invoke Medea's aid. The same idea had already occurred to Chalciope herself; but she had hesitated. On the one hand, she was afraid of failure: Medea might be so appalled by thoughts of her father's wrath that all entreaties would fall upon deaf ears. On the other, she feared that if her sister yielded to her prayers the whole conspiracy would be laid bare.

Meanwhile the maiden lay on her bed, fast asleep, with all her cares forgotten. But not for long. Dreams assailed her, deceitful dreams, the nightmares of a soul in pain. She dreamt that the stranger had accepted the challenge, not in the hope of winning the ram's fleece – it was not that that had brought him to Aea – but in order that he might carry her off to his own home as his bride. Then it seemed that it was she who was standing up to the bulls; she found it easy to handle them. But when all was done, her parents backed out of the bargain, pointing out that

23

it was Jason, not their daughter, whom they had dared to yoke the bulls. This led to an interminable dispute between her father and the Argonauts, which resulted in their leaving the decision to her – she could do as she pleased. And she, without a moment's thought, turned her back on her parents and chose the stranger. Her parents were cut to the quick; they screamed in their anger; and with their cries she woke.

She sat up, shivering with fright, and peered round the walls of her bedroom. Slowly and painfully she dragged herself back to reality. Then in self-pity she cried out and voiced the terror that her nightmare had engendered:

'These noblemen, their coming here, I fear it spells catastrophe. And how I tremble for their leader! He should pay court to some Achaean girl far away in his own country, leaving me content with spinsterhood and home. Ah no! Away with modesty! I will stand aside no longer; I will go to my sister. She is anxious for her sons and well might ask me for my help in the ordeal. And so my heartache would be eased.'

With that she rose, and in her gown, with nothing on her feet, went to her bedroom door and opened it. She was resolved to go to her sister and she crossed the threshold. But once outside she stayed for a long time where she was, inhibited by shame. Then she turned and went back into the room. Again she came out of it, and again she crept back, borne to and fro on hesitating feet.

Whenever she set out shame held her back; and all the time shame held her in the room shameless desire kept urging her to leave it. Three times she tried to go; three times she failed; and at the fourth attempt she threw herself face downward on the bed and writhed in pain.

Her plight was like that of a bride mourning in her bedroom for the young husband chosen for her by her brothers and parents, and lost by some stroke of Fate before the pair had enjoyed each other's love. Too shy and circumspect as yet to mingle freely with the maids and risk an unkind word or tactless jibe, she sits disconsolate in a corner of the room, looks at the empty bed and weeps in silence though her heart is bursting. Thus Medea wept.

But presently one of the servants, her own young maid, came to the room, and seeing her mistress lying there in tears, ran off to tell Chalciope, who was sitting with her sons considering how they might win Medea over. Chalciope did not make light of the girl's story, strange as it seemed. In great alarm she hurried through the house from her own to her sister's room, and there she found her lying in misery on the bed with both cheeks torn and her eyes red with weeping.

'My dear!' she cried. 'What is the meaning of these tears? What has made you so terribly unhappy? Have you suddenly been taken ill? Or has Father told you of some awful fate he has in mind for me and my sons? Oh, how

I wish I might never see this city and this home of ours again, and live at the world's end, where nobody has even heard of the Colchians!'

Medea blushed. She was eager to answer, but for a long while was checked by maiden modesty. Time and again the truth was on the tip of her tongue, only to be swallowed back. Time and again it tried to force a passage through her lovely lips, but no words came. At last, impelled by the bold hand of Love, she gave her sister a disingenuous reply: 'Chalciope, I am terrified for your sons. I am afraid that Father will destroy them out of hand, strangers and all. I had a little sleep just now and in a nightmare that is what I saw. God forfend such evil! May you never have to suffer so through them!'

Medea was trying to induce her sister to make the first move and appeal to her to save her sons. And indeed Chalciope was overwhelmed by horror at her disclosure. She said: 'My fears have been the same as yours. That is what brought me here. I hoped that you and I might put our heads together and find a way of rescuing my sons. But swear by Earth and Heaven that you will keep what I say to yourself and work in league with me. I implore you, by the happy gods, by your own head, and by your parents, not to stand by while they are mercilessly done to death. If you do so, may I die with my dear sons and haunt you afterwards from Hades like an avenging Fury.'

With that she burst into tears, sank down, and throwing her arms round her sister's knees buried her head in her lap. Each of them wailed in pity for the other, and faint sounds of women weeping in distress were heard throughout the palace.

Medea was the first to speak. 'Sister,' she said, 'you left me speechless when you talked of curses and avenging Furies. How can I set your mind at rest? I only wish we could be sure of rescuing your sons. However, I will do as you ask and take the solemn oath of the Colchians, swearing by mighty Heaven and by Earth below, the Mother of the Gods, that provided your demands are not impossible I will help you as you wish, with all the power that in me lies.'

When Medea had taken the oath, Chalciope said: 'Well now, for the sake of my sons, could you not devise some stratagem, some cunning ruse that the stranger could rely on in his trial? He needs you just as much as they do. In fact he has sent Argus here to urge me to enlist your help. I left him in the palace when I came to you just now.'

At this, Medea's heart leapt up. Her lovely cheeks were crimsoned and her eyes grew dim with tears of joy. 'Chalciope,' she cried, 'I will do anything to please you and your sons, anything to make you happy. May I never see the light of dawn again and may you see me in the world no more, if I put anything before your safety and the lives of your sons, who are my brothers, my dear kinsmen, with whom I was brought up. And you, am I not as much your daughter as your sister, you that took me to your breast

27

as you did them, when I was a baby, as I often heard my mother say? But go now and tell no one of my promise, so that my parents may not know how I propose to keep it. And at dawn I will go to Hecate's temple with magic medicine for the bulls.'

Thus assured, Chalciope withdrew from her sister's room and brought her sons the news of her success. But Medea, left alone, fell a prey once more to shame and horror at the way in which she planned to help a man in defiance of her father's wishes.

Night threw her shadow on the world. Sailors out at sea looked up at the circling Bear and the stars of Orion. Travellers and watchmen longed for sleep, and oblivion came at last to mothers mourning for their children's death. In the town, dogs ceased to bark and men to call to one another; silence reigned over the deepening dark. But gentle sleep did not visit Medea. In her yearning for Jason, fretful cares kept her awake. She feared the great strength of the bulls; she saw him face them in the field of Ares; she saw him meet an ignominious end. Her heart fluttered within her, restless as a patch of sunlight dancing up and down on a wall as the swirling water poured into a pail reflects it.

Tears of pity ran down her cheeks and her whole body was possessed by agony, a searing pain which shot along her nerves and deep into the nape of her neck, that vulnerable spot where the relentless archery of Love causes the keenest pangs. At one moment she thought she would give him the magic drug for the bulls; at the next she thought no, she would rather die herself; and then that she would do neither, but patiently endure her fate. In the end she sat down and debated with herself in miserable indecision:

'Evil on this side, evil on that; and must I choose between them? In either case my plight is desperate and there is no escape; this torture will go on. Oh how I wish that Artemis with her swift darts had put an end to me before I had seen that man, before Chalciope's sons had gone to Achaea! Some god, some Fury rather, must have brought them back with grief and tears for us. Let him be killed in the struggle, if it is indeed his fate to perish in the unploughed field. For how could I prepare the drug without my parents' knowledge? What story shall I tell them? What trickery will serve? How can I help him, and fail to be found out? Are he and I to meet alone? Indeed I am ill-starred, for even if he dies I have no hope of happiness; with Jason dead, I should taste real misery. Away with modesty, farewell to my good name! Saved from all harm by me, let him go where he pleases, and let me die. On the very day of his success I could hang myself from a rafter or take a deadly poison. Yet even so my death would never save me from their wicked tongues. My fate would be the talk of every city in the world; and here the Colchian women would bandy my name about and drag it in mud – the girl who fancied a foreigner enough to die for him, disgraced her parents and her home, went off her head for love. What infamy would not be mine? Ah, how I grieve now for the folly of my passion! Better to die here in my room this very night, passing from life unnoticed, unreproached, than to carry through this horrible, this despicable scheme.'

With that she went and fetched the box in which she kept her many drugs, healing or deadly, and putting it on her knees she wept. Tears ran unchecked in torrents down her cheeks and drenched her lap as she bemoaned her own sad destiny. She was determined now to take a poison from the box and swallow it; and in a moment she was fumbling with the fastening of the lid in her unhappy eagerness to reach the fatal drug. But suddenly she was overcome by the hateful thought of death, and for a long time she stayed her hand in silent horror. Visions of life and all its fascinating cares rose up before her. She thought of the pleasures that the living can enjoy. She thought of her happy playmates, as a young girl will. And now, setting its true value on all this, it seemed to her a sweeter thing to see the sun than it had ever been before. So, prompted by Here, she changed her mind and put the box away. Irresolute no longer, she waited eagerly for Dawn to come, so that she could meet the stranger face to face and give him the magic drug as she had promised. Time after time she opened her door to catch the first glimmer of day; and she rejoiced when early Dawn lit up the sky and people in the town began to stir.

Argus left the palace and returned to the ship. But he

told his brothers to wait before following him, in order to find out what Medea meant to do. She herself, as soon as she saw the first light of day, gathered up the golden locks that were floating round her shoulders in disorder, washed the stains from her cheeks and cleansed her skin with an ointment clear as nectar; then she put on a beautiful robe equipped with cunning brooches, and threw a silvery veil over her lovely head. And as she moved about, there in her own home, she walked oblivious of all evils imminent, and worse to come.

She had twelve maids, young as herself and all unmarried, who slept in the ante-chamber of her own sweet-scented room. She called them now and told them to yoke the mules to her carriage at once, as she wished to drive to the splendid Temple of Hecate; and while they were getting the carriage ready she took a magic ointment from her box. This salve was named after Prometheus. A man had only to smear it on his body, after propitiating the only-begotten Maiden with a midnight offering, to become invulnerable by sword or fire and for that day to surpass himself in strength and daring. It first appeared in a plant that sprang from the blood-like ichor of Prometheus in his torment, which the flesh-eating eagle had dropped on the spurs of Caucasus. The flowers, which grew on twin stalks a cubit high, were of the colour of Corycian saffron, while the root looked like flesh that has just been cut, and the juice like the dark sap of a mountain oak. To make the ointment, Medea, clothed in black, in the gloom of night, had drawn off this juice in a Caspian shell after bathing in seven perennial streams and calling seven times on Brimo, nurse of youth, Brimo, night-wanderer of the underworld, Queen of the dead. The dark earth shook and rumbled underneath the Titan root when it was cut, and Prometheus himself groaned in the anguish of his soul.

Such was the salve that Medea chose. Placing it in the fragrant girdle that she wore beneath her bosom, she left the house and got into her carriage, with two maids on either side. They gave her the reins, and taking the well-made whip in her right hand, she drove off through the town, while the rest of the maids tucked up their skirts above their white knees and ran behind along the broad highway, holding on to the wicker body of the carriage.

I see her there like Artemis, standing in her golden chariot after she has bathed in the gentle waters of Parthenius or the streams of Amnisus, and driving off with her fast-trotting deer over the hills and far away to some rich-scented sacrifice. Attendant nymphs have gathered at the source of Amnisus or flocked in from the glens and upland springs to follow her; and fawning beasts whimper in homage and tremble as she passes by. Thus Medea and her maids sped through the town, and on either side people made way for her, avoiding the princess's eye.

Leaving the city and its well-paved streets, she drove across the plain and drew up at the shrine. There she got quickly down from her smooth-running carriage and addressed her maids. 'My friends,' she said, 'I have done wrong. I forgot that we were told not to go among these foreigners who are wandering about the place. Everybody in the town is terrified, and in consequence none of the women who every day foregather here have come. But since we are here and it looks as though we shall be left in peace, we need not deny ourselves a little pleasure. Let us sing to our heart's content, and then, when we have gathered some of the lovely flowers in the meadow there, go back to town at the usual time. And if you will only fall in with a scheme of mine, you shall have something better than flowers to take home with you today. I will explain. Argus and Chalciope herself have persuaded me against my better judgement – but not a word to anyone of what I say; my father must not hear about it. They wish me to protect that stranger, the one who took up the challenge, in his mortal combat with the bulls and take some presents from him in return. I told them I thought well of the idea; and I have in fact invited him to come and see me here without his followers. But if he brings his gifts and hands them over, I mean to share them out among ourselves; and what we give him in return will be a deadlier drug than he expects. All I ask of you when he arrives is to leave me by myself.'

With this ingenious figment Medea satisfied her maids. Meanwhile Argus, when his brothers had told him she was going to the Temple of Hecate at dawn, drew Jason apart and conducted him across the plain. Mopsus son of Ampycus went with them, an excellent adviser for travellers setting out, and able to interpret any omen that a bird might offer on the way. As for Jason, by the grace of Here Queen of Heaven, no hero of the past, no son of Zeus himself, no offspring of the other gods, could have outshone him on that day, he was so good to look at, so delightful to talk to. Even his companions, as they glanced at him, were fascinated by his radiant charm. For Mopsus, it was a pleasurable journey: he had a shrewd idea how it would end.

Near the shrine and beside the path they followed, there stood a poplar, flaunting its myriad leaves. It was much frequented as a roost by garrulous crows, one of which flapped its wings as they were passing by, and cawing from the treetop expressed the sentiments of Here:

'Who is this inglorious seer who has not had the sense to realize, what even children know, that a girl does not permit herself to say a single word of love to a young man who brings an escort with him? Off with you, foolish prophet and incompetent diviner! You certainly are not inspired by Cypris or the gentle Loves.'

Mopsus listened to the bird's remarks with a smile at the reprimand from Heaven. Turning to Jason, he said: 'Proceed, my lord, to the temple, where you will find Medea and be graciously received, thanks to Aphrodite, who will be your ally in the hour of trial, as was foretold to us by Phineus son of Agenor. We two, Argus and I, will not go any nearer, but will wait here till you come back. You must go to her alone and attach her to yourself by your own persuasive eloquence.' This was sound advice and they both accepted it at once.

Meanwhile Medea, though she was singing and dancing with her maids, could think of one thing only. There was no melody, however gay, that did not quickly cease to please. Time and again she faltered and came to a halt. To keep her eyes fixed on her choir was more than she could do. She was for ever turning them aside to search the distant paths, and more than once she well-nigh fainted when she mistook the noise of the wind for the footfall of a passer-by.

But it was not so very long before the sight of Jason rewarded her impatient watch. Like Sirius rising from Ocean, brilliant and beautiful but full of menace for the flocks, he sprang into view, splendid to look at but fraught with trouble for the lovesick girl. Her heart stood still, a mist descended on her eyes, and a warm flush spread across her cheeks. She could neither move towards him nor retreat; her feet were rooted to the ground. And now her servants disappeared, and the pair of them stood face to face without a word or sound, like oaks or tall pines that stand in the mountains side by side in silence when the air is still, but when the wind has stirred them chatter without end. So these two, stirred by the breath of Love, were soon to pour out all their tale.

Jason, seeing how distraught Medea was, tried to put her at her ease. 'Lady,' he said, 'I am alone. Why are you so fearful of me? I am not a profligate as some men are, and never was, even in my own country. So you have no need to be on your guard, but may ask or tell me anything you wish. We have come together here as friends, in a consecrated spot which must not be profaned. Speak to me, question me, without reserve; and since you have already promised your sister to give me the talisman I need so much, pray do not put me off with pleasant speeches. I plead to you by Hecate herself, by your parents, and by Zeus. His hand protects all suppliants and strangers, and I that now address my prayers to you in my necessity am both a stranger and a suppliant. Without you and your sister I shall never succeed in my appalling task. Grant me your aid and in the days to come I will reward you duly, repaying you as best I can from the distant land where I shall sing your praises. My comrades too when they are back in Hellas will immortalize your name. So will their wives and mothers, whom I think of now as sitting by the sea, shedding tears in their anxiety for us – bitter tears, which you could wipe away. Remember Ariadne, young Ariadne, daughter of Minos and Pasiphae, who was a daughter of the Sun. She did not scruple to befriend Theseus and save him in his hour of trial; and then, when Minos had relented, she left her home and sailed away with him. She was the darling of the gods and she has her emblem in the sky: all night a ring of stars called Ariadne's Crown rolls on its way among the heavenly constellations. You too will be thanked by the gods if you save me and all my noble friends. Indeed your loveliness assures me of a kind and tender heart within.'

Jason's homage melted Medea. Turning her eyes aside she smiled divinely and then, uplifted by his praise, she looked him in the face. How to begin, she did not know; she longed so much to tell him everything at once. But with the charm, she did not hesitate; she drew it out from her sweet-scented girdle and he took it in his hands with joy. She revelled in his need of her and would have poured out all her soul to him as well, so captivating was the light of love that streamed from Jason's golden head and held her gleaming eyes. Her heart was warmed and melted like the dew on roses under the morning sun.

At one moment both of them were staring at the ground in deep embarrassment; at the next they were smiling and glancing at each other with the love-light in their eyes. But at last Medea forced herself to speak to him. 'Hear me now,' she said. 'These are my plans for you. When you have met my father and he has given you the deadly teeth from the serpent's jaws, wait for the moment of midnight and after bathing in an ever-running river, go out alone in sombre clothes and dig a round pit in the earth. There, kill a ewe and after heaping up a pyre over the pit, sacrifice it whole, with a libation of honey from the hive and prayers to Hecate, Perses' only Daughter. Then, when you have invoked the goddess duly, withdraw from the pyre. And do not be tempted to look behind you as you go,

37

either by footfalls or the baying of hounds, or you may ruin everything and never reach your friends alive.

'In the morning, melt this charm, strip, and using it like oil, anoint your body. It will endow you with tremendous strength and boundless confidence. You will feel yourself a match, not for mere men, but for the gods themselves. Sprinkle your spear and shield and sword with it as well; and neither the spear-points of the earth-born men nor the consuming flames that the savage bulls spew out will find you vulnerable. But you will not be immune for long – only for the day. Nevertheless, do not at any moment flinch from the encounter.

'And here is something else that will stand you in good stead. You have yoked the mighty bulls; you have ploughed the stubborn fallow (with those great hands and all that strength it will not take you long); you have sown the serpent's teeth in the dark earth; and now the giants are springing up along the furrows. Watch till you see a number of them rise from the soil, then, before they see you, throw a great boulder in among them; and they will fall it like famished dogs and kill one another. That is your moment; plunge into the fray yourself.

'And so the task is done and you can carry off the fleece to Hellas – a long, long way from Aea, I believe. Go none the less, go where you will; go where the fancy takes you when you part from us.'

After this, Medea was silent for a while. She kept her eyes fixed on the ground, and the warm tears ran down her lovely cheeks as she saw him sailing off over the high seas far away from her. Then she looked up at him and sorrowfully spoke again, taking his right hand in hers and no longer attempting to conceal her love. She said:

'But do remember, if you ever reach your home. Remember the name of Medea, and I for my part will remember you when you are far away. But now, pray tell me where you live. Where are you bound for when you sail across the sea from here? Will your journey take you near the wealthy city of Orchomenus or the Isle of Aea? Tell me too about that girl you mentioned, who won such fame for herself, the daughter of Pasiphae my father's sister.'

As he listened to this and noted her tears, unconscionable Love stole into the heart of Jason too. He replied: 'Of one thing I am sure. If I escape and live to reach Achaea; if Aeëtes does not set us a still more formidable task; never by night or day shall I forget you. But you asked about the country of my birth. If it pleases you to hear, I will describe it; indeed I should like nothing better. It is a land ringed by lofty mountains, rich in sheep and pasture, and the birthplace of Prometheus' son, the good Deucalion, who was the first man to found cities, build temples to the gods and rule mankind as king. Its neighbours call the land Haemonia, and in it stands Iolcus, my own town, and many others too where the very name of the Aeaean Island is unknown. Yet they do say that it was from these parts that the Aeolid Minyas migrated long ago to found Orchomenus, which borders on Cadmeian lands. But why do I trouble you with all this tiresome talk about my home and Minos' daughter, the far-famed Ariadne, that lovely lady with the glorious name who roused your curiosity? I can only hope that, as Minos came to terms with Theseus for her sake, your father will be reconciled with us.'

He had thought, by talking in this gentle way, to soothe Medea. But she was now obsessed by the gloomiest forebodings; embittered too. And she answered him with passion:

'No doubt in Hellas people think it right to honour their agreements. But Aeëtes is not the kind of man that Minos was, if what you say of him is true; and as for Ariadne, I cannot claim to be a match for her. So do not talk of friendliness to strangers. But oh, at least remember me when you are back in Iolcus; and I, despite my parents, will remember you. And may there come to me some whisper from afar, some bird to tell the tale, when you forget me. Or may the Storm-Winds snatch me up and carry me across the sea to Iolcus, to denounce you to your face and remind you that I saved your life. That is the moment I would choose to pay an unexpected visit to your house.'

As she spoke, tears of misery ran down her cheeks. But Jason said: 'Dear lady, you may spare the wandering Winds that task, and your tell-tale bird as well, for you are talking nonsense. If you come to us in Hellas you will be honoured and revered by both the women and the men. Indeed they will treat you as a goddess, because it was through you that their sons came home alive, or their brothers, kinsmen, or beloved husbands were saved from hurt. And there shall be a bridal bed for you, which you and I will share. Nothing shall part us in our love till Death at his appointed hour removes us from the light of day.'

As she heard these words of his, her heart melted within her. And yet she shuddered as she thought of the disastrous step she was about to take. Poor girl! She was not going to refuse for long this offer of a home in Hellas. The goddess Here had arranged it all: Medea was to leave her native land for the sacred city of Iolcus, and there to bring his punishment to Pelias.

Her maids, who had been spying on them from afar, were now becoming restive, though they did not intervene. It was high time for the maiden to go home to her mother. But Medea had no thought of leaving yet; she was entranced both by his comeliness and his bewitching talk. At last however, Jason, who had kept his wits about him, said, 'Now we must part, or the sun will set before we know it. Besides, some passer-by might see us. But we will meet each other here again.'

By gentle steps they had advanced so far towards an understanding. And now they parted, he in a joyful mood to go back to his companions and the ship, she to rejoin her maids, who all ran up to meet her. But as they gathered round, she did not even notice them: her head was in the clouds. Without knowing what she did, she got into her carriage to drive the mules, taking the reins in one hand and the whip in the other. And off they trotted to the palace in the town.

She had no sooner arrived than Chalciope questioned her anxiously about her sons. But Medea had left her wits behind her. She neither heard a word her sister said nor showed the least desire to answer her inquiries. She sat down on a low stool at the foot of her bed, leant over and rested her cheek on her left hand, pondering with tears in her eyes on the infamous part she had played in a scene that she herself had staged.

Jason found his escort in the place where he had left them, and as they set out to rejoin the rest, he told them how he had fared. When the party reached the ship, he was received with open arms and in reply to the questions of his friends he told them of Medea's plans and showed them the powerful charm. Idas was the only member of the company who was not impressed. He sat aloof, nursing his resentment. The rest were overjoyed, and since the night permitted no immediate move, they settled down in peace and comfort. But at dawn they despatched two men to Aeetes to ask him for the seed, Telamon beloved of Ares, and Aethalides the famous son of Hermes. This pair set out on their errand, and they did not fail. When they reached the king, he handed them the deadly teeth that Jason was to sow.

The teeth were those of the Aonian serpent, the guardian of Ares' spring, which Cadmus killed in Ogygian Thebes. He had come there in his search for Europa, and there he settled, under the guidance of a heifer picked out for him by Apollo in an oracle. Athene, Lady of Trito, tore the teeth out of the serpent's jaws and divided them between Aeëtes and Cadmus, the slayer of the beast. Cadmus sowed them in the Aonian plain and founded an earthborn clan with all that had escaped the spear of Ares when he did his harvesting. Such were the teeth that Aeëtes let them take back to the ship. He gave them willingly, as he was satisfied that Jason, even if he yoked the bulls, would prove unable to finish off the task.

It was evening. Out in the west, beyond the farthest Ethiopian hills, the Sun was sinking under the darkening world; Night was harnessing her team; and the Argonauts were preparing their beds by the hawsers of the ship. But Jason waited for the bright constellation of the Bear to decline, and then, when all the air from heaven to earth was still, he set out like a stealthy thief across the solitary plain. During the day he had prepared himself, and so had everything he needed with him; Argus had fetched him some milk and a ewe from a farm; the rest he had taken from the ship itself. When he had found an unfrequented spot in a clear meadow under the open sky, he began by bathing his naked body reverently in the sacred river, and then put on a dark mantle which Hypsipyle of Lemnos had given him to remind him of their passionate

43

embraces. Then he dug a pit a cubit deep, piled up billets, and laid the sheep on top of them after cutting its throat. He kindled the wood from underneath and poured mingled libations on the sacrifice, calling on Hecate Brimo to help him in the coming test. This done, he withdrew; and the dread goddess, hearing his words from the abyss, came up to accept the offering of Aeson's son. She was garlanded by fearsome snakes that coiled themselves round twigs of oak; the twinkle of a thousand torches lit the scene; and hounds of the underworld barked shrilly all around her. The whole meadow trembled under her feet, and the nymphs of marsh and river who haunt the fens by Amarantian Phasis cried out in fear. Jason was terrified; but even so, as he retreated, he did not once turn round. And so he found himself among his friends once more, and Dawn arrived, showing herself betimes above the snows of Caucasus.

At daybreak too, Aeëtes put on his breast the stiff cuirass which Ares had given him after slaying Mimas with his own hands in the field of Phlegra; and on his head he set his golden helmet with its four plates, bright as the Sun's round face when he rises fresh from Ocean Stream. And he took up his shield of many hides, and his unconquerable spear, a spear that none of the Argonauts could have withstood, now that they had deserted Heracles, who alone could have dealt with it in battle. Phaëthon was close at hand, holding his father's swift horses and well-built chariot in readiness. Aeëtes mounted, took the reins in his hands, and drove out of the town along the broad highway to attend the contest, followed by hurrying crowds. Lord of the Colchians, he might have been Poseidon in his chariot driving to the Isthmian Games, to Taenarum, to the waters of Lerna, or through the grove of Onchestus, and on to Calaurea with his steeds, to the Haemonian Rock or the woods of Geraestus.

Meanwhile Jason, remembering Medea's instructions, melted the magic drug and sprinkled his shield with it and his sturdy spear and sword. His comrades watched him and put his weapons to the proof with all the force they had. But they could not bend the spear at all; even in their strong hands it proved itself unbreakable. Idas was furious with them. He hacked at the butt-end of the spear with his great sword, but the blade rebounded from it like a hammer from the anvil. And a great shout of joy went up; they felt that the battle was already won.

Next, Jason sprinkled his own body and was imbued with miraculous, indomitable might. As his hands increased in power, his very fingers twitched. Like a war-horse eager for battle, pawing the ground, neighing, pricking its ears and tossing up its head in pride, he exulted in the strength of his limbs. Time and again he leapt high in the air this way and that, brandishing his shield of bronze and ashen spear. The weapons flashed on the eye like intermittent lightning playing in a stormy sky from black clouds charged with rain.

After that there was no faltering; the Argonauts were

ready for the test. They took their places on the benches
of the ship and rowed her swiftly upstream to the plain
of Ares. This lay as far beyond the city as a chariot has to
travel from start to turning-post when the kinsmen of a
dead king are holding foot and chariot races in his honour. They found Aeëtes there and a full gathering of the
Colchians. The tribesmen were stationed on the rocky
spurs of Caucasus, and the king was wheeling around in
his chariot on the river-bank.

Jason, as soon as his men had made the hawsers fast,
leapt from the ship and entered the lists with spear and
shield. He also took with him a shining bronze helmet
full of sharp teeth, and his sword was slung from his
shoulder. But his body was bare, so that he looked like
Apollo of the golden sword as much as Ares god of war.
Glancing round the field, he saw the bronze yoke for the
bulls and beside it the plough of indurated steel, all in
one piece. He went up to them, planted his heavy spear
in the ground by its butt and laid the helmet down, lean-
ing it against the spear. Then he went forward with his
shield alone to examine the countless tracks that the bulls
had made. And now, from somewhere in the bowels of
the earth, from the smoky stronghold where they slept,
the pair of bulls appeared, breathing flames of fire. The
Argonauts were terrified at the sight. But Jason planting
his feet apart stood to receive them, as a reef in the sea
confronts the tossing billows in a gale. He held his shield

in front of him, and the two bulls, bellowing loudly, charged and butted it with their strong horns. But he was not shifted from his stance, not by so much as an inch. The bulls snorted and spurted from their mouths devouring flames, like a perforated crucible when the leather bellows of the smith, sometimes ceasing, sometimes blowing hard, have made a blaze and the fire leaps up from below with a terrific roar. The deadly heat assailed him on all sides with the force of lightning. But he was protected by Medea's magic. Seizing the right-hand bull by the tip of its horn, he dragged it with all his might towards the yoke, and then brought it down on its knees with a sudden kick on its bronze foot. The other charged, and was felled in the same way at a single blow; and Jason, who had cast his shield aside, stood with his feet apart, and though the flames at once enveloped him, held them both down on their fore-knees where they fell. Aeëtes marvelled at the man's strength.

Castor and Polydeuces picked up the yoke and gave it to Jason – they had been detailed for the task and were close at hand. Jason bound it tight on the bulls' necks, lifted the bronze pole between them and fastened it to the yoke by its pointed end, while the Twins backed out of the heat and returned to the ship. Then, taking his shield from the ground he slung it on his back, picked up the heavy helmet full of teeth and grasped his unconquerable spear, with which, like some ploughman using his Pelasgian goad, he pricked the bulls under their flanks and with a firm grip on its well-made handle guided the adamantine plough.

At first the bulls in their high fury spurted flames of fire. Their breath came out with a roar like that of the blustering wind that causes frightened mariners to take in sail. But presently, admonished by the spear, they went ahead, and the rough fallow cleft by their own and the great ploughman's might lay broken up behind them. The huge clods as they were torn away along the furrow groaned aloud; and Jason came behind, planting his feet down firmly on the field. As he ploughed he sowed the teeth, casting them far from himself with many a backward glance lest a deadly crop of earthborn men should catch him unawares. And the bulls, thrusting their bronze hoofs into the earth, toiled on till only a third of the passing day was left. Then, when weary labourers in other fields were hoping it would soon be time to free their oxen from the yoke, this indefatigable ploughman's work was done – the whole four-acre field was ploughed.

Jason freed his bulls from the plough and shooed them off. They fled across the plain; and he, seeing that no earthborn men had yet appeared in the furrows, seized the occasion to go back to the ship, where his comrades gathered round him with heartening words. He dipped his helmet in the flowing river and with its water quenched his thirst, then flexed his knees to keep them supple; and as fresh courage filled his heart, he lashed himself into a fury, like a wild boar when it whets its teeth to face the hunt and the foam drips to the ground from its savage mouth.

By now the earthborn men were shooting up like corn in all parts of the field. The deadly War-god's sacred plot bristled with stout shields, double-pointed spears, and glittering helmets. The splendour of it flashed through the air above and struck Olympus. Indeed this army springing from the earth shone out like the full congregation of the stars piercing the darkness of a murky night, when snow lies deep and the winds have chased the wintry clouds away. But Jason did not forget the counsel he had had from Medea of the many wiles. He picked up from the field a huge round boulder, a formidable quoit that Ares might have thrown, but four strong men together could not have budged from its place. Rushing forward with this in his hands he hurled it far away among the earthborn men, then crouched behind his shield, unseen and full of confidence. The Colchians gave a mighty shout like the roar of the sea beating on jagged rocks; and the king himself was astounded as he saw the great quoit hurtle through the air. But the earthborn men, like nimble hounds, leapt on one another and with loud yells began to slay. Beneath each other's spears they fell on their mother earth, as pines or oaks are blown down by a gale. And now, like a bright meteor that leaps from heaven and leaves a fiery trail behind it, portentous to all those who see it flash across the night, the son of Aeson hurled

himself on them with his sword unsheathed and in pro-
miscuous slaughter mowed them down, striking as he
could, for many of them had but half emerged and
showed their flanks and bellies only, some had their
shoulders clear, some had just stood up, and others were
afoot already and rushing into battle. So might some
farmer threatened by a frontier war snatch up a newly
sharpened sickle and, lest the enemy should reap his fields
before him, hasten to cut down the unripe corn, not wait-
ing for the season and the sun to ripen it. Thus Jason cut
his crop of earthborn men. Blood filled the furrows as
water fills the conduits of a spring. And still they fell,
some on their faces biting the rough clods, some on their
backs, and others on their hands and sides, looking like
monsters from the sea. Many were struck before they
could lift up their feet, and rested there with the death-dew
on their brows, each trailing on the earth so much of him
as had come up into the light of day. They lay like saplings
in an orchard bowed to the ground when Zeus has sent
torrential rain and snapped them at the root, wasting the
gardeners' toil and bringing heartbreak to the owner of
the plot, the man who planted them.

Such was the scene that King Aeëtes now surveyed, and
such his bitterness. He went back to the city with his
Colchians, pondering on the quickest way to bring the
foreigners to book. And the sun sank and Jason's task was
done.

1. BOCCACCIO · *Mrs Rosie and the Priest*
2. GERARD MANLEY HOPKINS · *As kingfishers catch fire*
3. *The Saga of Gunnlaug Serpent-tongue*
4. THOMAS DE QUINCEY · *On Murder Considered as One of the Fine Arts*
5. FRIEDRICH NIETZSCHE · *Aphorisms on Love and Hate*
6. JOHN RUSKIN · *Traffic*
7. PU SONGLING · *Wailing Ghosts*
8. JONATHAN SWIFT · *A Modest Proposal*
9. *Three Tang Dynasty Poets*
10. WALT WHITMAN · *On the Beach at Night Alone*
11. KENKŌ · *A Cup of Sake Beneath the Cherry Trees*
12. BALTASAR GRACIÁN · *How to Use Your Enemies*
13. JOHN KEATS · *The Eve of St Agnes*
14. THOMAS HARDY · *Woman much missed*
15. GUY DE MAUPASSANT · *Femme Fatale*
16. MARCO POLO · *Travels in the Land of Serpents and Pearls*
17. SUETONIUS · *Caligula*
18. APOLLONIUS OF RHODES · *Jason and Medea*
19. ROBERT LOUIS STEVENSON · *Olalla*
20. KARL MARX AND FRIEDRICH ENGELS · *The Communist Manifesto*
21. PETRONIUS · *Trimalchio's Feast*
22. JOHANN PETER HEBEL · *How a Ghastly Story Was Brought to Light by a Common or Garden Butcher's Dog*
23. HANS CHRISTIAN ANDERSEN · *The Tinder Box*
24. RUDYARD KIPLING · *The Gate of the Hundred Sorrows*
25. DANTE · *Circles of Hell*
26. HENRY MAYHEW · *Of Street Piemen*
27. HAFEZ · *The nightingales are drunk*
28. GEOFFREY CHAUCER · *The Wife of Bath*
29. MICHEL DE MONTAIGNE · *How We Weep and Laugh at the Same Thing*
30. THOMAS NASHE · *The Terrors of the Night*
31. EDGAR ALLAN POE · *The Tell-Tale Heart*
32. MARY KINGSLEY · *A Hippo Banquet*
33. JANE AUSTEN · *The Beautifull Cassandra*
34. ANTON CHEKHOV · *Gooseberries*
35. SAMUEL TAYLOR COLERIDGE · *Well, they are gone, and here must I remain*
36. JOHANN WOLFGANG VON GOETHE · *Sketchy, Doubtful, Incomplete Jottings*
37. CHARLES DICKENS · *The Great Winglebury Duel*
38. HERMAN MELVILLE · *The Maldive Shark*
39. ELIZABETH GASKELL · *The Old Nurse's Story*
40. NIKOLAY LESKOV · *The Steel Flea*

41. HONORÉ DE BALZAC · *The Atheist's Mass*
42. CHARLOTTE PERKINS GILMAN · *The Yellow Wall-Paper*
43. C.P. CAVAFY · *Remember, Body . . .*
44. FYODOR DOSTOEVSKY · *The Meek One*
45. GUSTAVE FLAUBERT · *A Simple Heart*
46. NIKOLAI GOGOL · *The Nose*
47. SAMUEL PEPYS · *The Great Fire of London*
48. EDITH WHARTON · *The Reckoning*
49. HENRY JAMES · *The Figure in the Carpet*
50. WILFRED OWEN · *Anthem For Doomed Youth*
51. WOLFGANG AMADEUS MOZART · *My Dearest Father*
52. PLATO · *Socrates' Defence*
53. CHRISTINA ROSSETTI · *Goblin Market*
54. *Sindbad the Sailor*
55. SOPHOCLES · *Antigone*
56. RYŪNOSUKE AKUTAGAWA · *The Life of a Stupid Man*
57. LEO TOLSTOY · *How Much Land Does A Man Need?*
58. GIORGIO VASARI · *Leonardo da Vinci*
59. OSCAR WILDE · *Lord Arthur Savile's Crime*
60. SHEN FU · *The Old Man of the Moon*
61. AESOP · *The Dolphins, the Whales and the Gudgeon*
62. MATSUO BASHŌ · *Lips too Chilled*
63. EMILY BRONTË · *The Night is Darkening Round Me*
64. JOSEPH CONRAD · *To-morrow*
65. RICHARD HAKLUYT · *The Voyage of Sir Francis Drake Around the Whole Globe*
66. KATE CHOPIN · *A Pair of Silk Stockings*
67. CHARLES DARWIN · *It was snowing butterflies*
68. BROTHERS GRIMM · *The Robber Bridegroom*
69. CATULLUS · *I Hate and I Love*
70. HOMER · *Circe and the Cyclops*
71. D. H. LAWRENCE · *Il Duro*
72. KATHERINE MANSFIELD · *Miss Brill*
73. OVID · *The Fall of Icarus*
74. SAPPHO · *Come Close*
75. IVAN TURGENEV · *Kasyan from the Beautiful Lands*
76. VIRGIL · *O Cruel Alexis*
77. H. G. WELLS · *A Slip under the Microscope*
78. HERODOTUS · *The Madness of Cambyses*
79. *Speaking of Siva*
80. *The Dhammapada*